HIDDEN
WITH CHRIST
IN GOD

I0555073

Richard Chandler

PRESTON SQUIRE
PUBLISHING

Produced by Preston Squire Publishing
46 Bell St
Barrie, ON
Canada L4N 0H9
prestonsquirepublishing.com

ISBNs: (print) 978-1-990078-12-5
(ebook) 978-1-990078-13-2

Table of Contents

FOREWORD

Sometime in the early years of my spiritual growth, I became fixated on the many accounts of how God brought victory for His people through a variety of personalities, ways, and means. I would listen to "sentiments of faith" expressed by the elders such as: "God is the same yesterday today and forever"; "Nothing is impossible with God", "Jesus never fails", and on and on. The more I heard these "expressions", the more I began to assess my own grasp of them and my desire to be able to go beyond just saying the words into actually believing them. I immersed myself in bible studies, bible reading, reading Christian material, prayer, church attendance, involvement in various church groups and duties, and attending Christian conventions of various kinds. God had placed within me a "hunger"!

I advanced to a point where I was not finding fulfilment, and out of a sense of frustration I asked God a question which, in hindsight, has led to a journey the fullness of which I am unable to fully express in writing. But as Holy Spirit has challenged me to do, I have included some aspects of it in these pages. The question I am alluding to is: "Is this all there is?"

I would point out, without hesitation, that I have learned (through much trial and error) not to judge another person's appetite for God, for which I am very thankful, especially given the lack of stress experienced as a result (especially pertaining to closest loved ones). The Word of God advises us to "work out our own salvation with fear and trembling". The manner in which we apply ourselves to the task is very much an individual choice. Holy Spirit will gladly guide us along the optimum path **if we choose to obey**. The difficulty, especially as a spouse and or parent, is learning how to "let go and let God". Which doesn't come easy, as having faith in God bolstered by confidence in his ability to keep, protect, and deliver those truly committed into his hands takes time to develop!

I express this sentiment because if one chooses to ask God the question "Is this all there is?" as pertains to Christianity, with a desire to actually discover the answer, the expression "fasten your seat belt" is the most appropriate I could ever think of! Each of us are different individuals and we each travel along different paths, and only God knows what it takes to "grow" us individually! I am learning that if you show God diligence and hunger, He will feed you limitlessly. If not, He will not force feed you. The choice is ours ("Blessed are those who hunger and thirst for righteousness for they will be filled" – Matthew 5:6 - NIV).

The path God chose for me thus far, that He might answer "the question", began with His calling me out of a 20-plus-year position of a very secure, well-paying job into job uncertainty and eventual joblessness for a time (the "stripping" had begun). I had never experienced being without a job – ever! Little did I realize at the time that the journey was just getting started, with much, much, much more to come! He had challenged me to format my resignation, which in itself was a monumental step of faith in my mind (I was thinking that He was just testing my obedience). However, when He told me to submit it, I was blown away. To be sure, my wife and I prayed long and hard over that one, but there was no doubt that He had spoken to me about it. Prior to calling me out of that specific job (that was the first), the

Lord gave me many scriptures and rhema words of comfort, and I have come to greatly cherish each of them as Holy Spirit has provided meaning and revelation. One of the initial rhema words He gave me, which has continuously comforted in the darkest of hours, is: "When you find that Jesus is all you've got, you will find that He is all you need"! The comfort provided by that word, combined with God's promise that His word will never return to him empty (Isaiah 55:11 - NIV), has kept and continues to keep me standing firm even, when I have felt like a flag attached to a flag pole in very strong winds. At the same time I received that word, He also directed me to Isaiah 7:9(NIV) – "If you do not stand firm in your faith, you will not stand at all".

God must have overcomers to work through, and the only way to become one is to be presented with that which we must learn to overcome (in His strength and by His direction, not our own. Indeed, He has cautioned us that "apart from Him we can do nothing")! He has also made it clear that without faith it is **impossible** to please Him! The major focus in learning to deal with the challenges is not just in overcoming them, but learning (along the way) total dependency on our never failing, merciful, compassionate, long suffering, patient, always faithful, awesome, loving God (David said: "**Taste** and see that the Lord is good – Psalm 34:8-NIV")! Also, as faith increases, we find that not only is learning to deal with the "challenges" important, but the attitude we display while doing so is monumental in that an attitude of "peace during the storm" is the best indicator of our learning to trust God. Additionally, as the words of the Apostle begin to truly register, namely 1 Peter 4:12(NIV) – "Dear friends, do not be surprised at the fiery ordeal that has to come on you to test you, **as though something strange were happening to you**"; the realization of the great value of getting to know Christ Jesus more and more begins to greatly overshadow the duration and intensity of the trials, along with the further realization that we are gaining valuable growth and insight into what being "Hidden with Christ in God" entails!

> Jer 17:7-8(NIV) – "But blessed is the one who trusts in the Lord, **whose confidence is in him**. They will be like a tree planted by the water that sends out its roots by the stream. It does not fear when the heat comes; its leaves are always green. It has no worries in a year of drought and never fails to bear fruit."

Lastly, my fervent prayer is that those who read this material will remain focused on Christ Jesus – not on the author!

APPROPRIATE FOCUS

Simply stated, I am fully persuaded that God's priority for the church (which has never changed, but has been ignored, misunderstood, misinterpreted, and misrepresented to our own loss) remains the crucifixion (complete elimination) of what God refers to as the flesh! There are numerous scriptures which highlight this and leave no wiggle room! The loss is on two fronts—individually and corporately. Individually in that we are not able to function according to God's design and purposes if the flesh is in ascendency to the Spirit. Corporately in that, as part of the body of Christ Jesus, we must be functioning appropriately as individuals in order to enable the body as a whole to function according to God's design. A vehicle, appliance, etc., which has a part that is not functioning as designed will not fully operate according to specifications!

> Consider Gal 5:24(NIV) – "Those who belong to Christ Jesus have crucified the flesh with its passions and desires". A very sobering scripture indeed, which should challenge any who reference themselves as Christian to check for any frivolity in making the claim (not based on self-analysis, but rather constantly looking to Holy Spirit for certification).

> Romans 8:1(KJ) – "Therefore there is now no condemnation to them which are in Christ Jesus, **who walk not after the flesh, but after the Spirit**".

Eph 4:11-16(NIV) – "So Christ himself gave the apostles, the prophets, the evangelists, the pastors and teachers to equip his people for works of service, so that the body of Christ might be built up until we all reach unity in the faith and in the knowledge of the Son of God and become mature, attaining to the whole measure of the fullness of Christ. Then we will no longer be infants, tossed back and forth by the waves, and blown here and there by every wind of teaching and by the cunning and craftiness of people in their deceitful scheming. Instead, speaking the truth in love, we will grow to become in every respect, the mature body of Him who is the head, that is, Christ. From him the whole body, joined and held together by every supporting ligament, grows and builds itself up in love, **AS EACH PART DOES ITS WORK."**

Romans 12:5(NIV) – "So in Christ we, though many, form one body, **AND EACH MEMBER BELONGS TO ALL THE OTHERS."**

We are called to a state of unity which is far beyond the level of superficiality which the majority of us have come to imagine or practice. That which God has called us to can only be achieved if we are willing to do our individual part to eliminate the flesh, which is a hindrance far beyond our comprehension! That calling indeed embraces eternity, but we need to realize that eternity begins for us in Christ – **while we walk this earthly sod**! There is no death in Christ. All we do is transition, leaving these earthly tents behind!

It is important, however, to always remember that crucifying the flesh is a process. Eliminating it is definitely not a once and done ordeal. Indeed, Jesus has instructed those who would strive to be His disciples that they must take up their cross daily! The success and pace of this day to day process is absolutely dependent upon our individual willingness to surrender (over time) to God, since we are only able to deal appropriately with the flesh with the guidance and help of Holy Spirit. We can be focused on "doing for Jesus" and lose sight of this as a priority. The journey of surrender takes time, as the Lord will place His finger on un-yielded areas of our lives and patiently help us to exercise the faith to allow Him (by His grace) to have His way. He won't force the issue, but in His loving way will grant understanding of the reasoning, **if we choose to work with Him**. Otherwise, the journey becomes plagued with stubbornness and the like, resulting in what will at times amount to significant loss of peace and joy, thereby making it an arduous journey. The God who advises us to "rejoice always; pray without ceasing; give thanks in all things;" (1 Thess 5:16-18(KJ)) has not ordained such. The choice is ours!

> Romans 8:13(NIV) – "For if you live according to the flesh you will die; but **IF BY THE SPIRIT** you put to death the misdeeds of the body, you will live."

It is crucial that we also comprehend the level of disdain (even hatred) that God has for what He refers to as flesh! A good place to start is to consider that God allowed His Son to be subjected to one of the worst forms of execution ever devised by man in the form of crucifixion (for our salvation), which was designed to extract every ounce of suffering short of death. To require such an end of something surely suggests a level of loathing beyond our comprehension! From another viewpoint, it also speaks to the depth of God's love, that He would allow His Son to be subjected to such an inhumane and violent death, as it is the only acceptable way for our holy, pure, and righteous God to be able to forgive us and to reconcile us to Himself through Christ Jesus. ("O the love that drew salvation's plan, O, the grace that brought it down to man, O, the mighty gulf that God did span at Calvary!")

The place where the things of God break down is at the point where we allow the carnal mind to try to make those things digestible for our intellect. 1 Cor 2:14(NIV) – "The person without the Spirit does not accept the things that come from the Spirit of God, but considers them foolishness, and cannot understand them because they are discerned only through the Spirit."

There can be no mistaking what God refers to as the works of the flesh (that which is in conflict with the Spirit):

- Gal 5:16-21(NIV) – "So I say, walk by the Spirit, and you will not gratify the desires of the flesh. For the flesh desires what is contrary to the Spirit, and the Spirit what is contrary to the flesh. They are in conflict with each other, so that you are not to do whatever you want. But if you are led by the Spirit, you are not under the law. **The acts of the flesh are obvious**: sexual immorality, impurity and debauchery, idolatry and witchcraft, hatred, discord, jealousy, fits of rage, selfish ambition, dissensions, factions and envy; drunkenness, orgies and the like. I warn you, as I did before that those who live like this will not inherit the Kingdom of God."

- 1 Peter 2:11(NIV) – "Dear friends, I urge you, as foreigners and exiles, to abstain from sinful desires, which wage war against your soul."

It is imperative, however, that we do recognize and acknowledge such things as they are—the "works" or "acts" of the flesh, and not the flesh itself which is the "self-life" otherwise referenced as the "I" in us.

> Gal 2:20(NIV) – "I have been crucified with Christ, and I no longer live, but Christ lives in me. The life I now live in the body, I live by faith in the Son of God, who loved me and gave himself for me."

Until the "I" in us is nailed to the cross, the "works of the flesh" will flourish; hence the reason for us to be completely surrendered in obedience to Holy Spirit, who alone can help us in our battle to overcome the "works of the flesh" as we deny the flesh **DAILY**, "take up our cross and follow him"! As with anything that is regularly denied nutrition, it will eventually meet its demise! Romans 13:14 KJ – "But put ye on the Lord Christ Jesus **and make no provision for the flesh**, to fulfill the lusts thereof." e.g. **don't feed that which you are trying to put to death.**"

As children in Sunday school, we often sang "Oh be careful little eyes what you see, oh be careful little eyes what you see, for the Father up above is looking down in love, so be careful little eyes what you see" (reference was also made to other parts of the anatomy i.e., ears, mouth, feet). We sang it without a great depth of understanding, of course. Certainly not fully grasping the fullness of how such actions would help to enable us to "**make no provision for the flesh**"!

Given the onslaught of ungodly material we have to deal with in this "advanced age", we need to consider the wisdom of making such simple truths a regular part of our daily spiritual diet! We also definitely need the wisdom and guidance of Holy Spirit in determining what He refers to as "ungodly" instead of making such determination on our own and potentially missing the mark completely!

As an aside, I have listened to discussions pertaining to whether we (in this era) are under grace or under the law. I choose to pay much heed to Gal 5:18(NIV) – "**But if you are led by the Spirit**, you are not under the law"! (Where does that place those who merely pay lip service as far as relationship with the blessed Holy Spirit is concerned?)

> Romans 8:8(KJ) – "So then they that are in the flesh cannot please God."

> Romans 8:14(NIV) – "For those who are led by the Spirit of God are the children of God."

> 1 Cor 9:26-27(NIV) – "Therefore I do not run like someone running aimlessly; I do not fight like a boxer beating the air. No, I strike a blow to my body and make it my slave so that after I have preached to others, I myself will not be disqualified for the prize."

Let us be always aware that God (a God of truth) does not accept or excuse artificiality or pretense on any level!

There is another scripture which addresses this matter of eliminating the flesh. Unfortunately, however, it seems to be referenced only at funerals. (Psalm 116:15(KJ)) – "Precious in the sight of the Lord is the death of his saints." I have great difficulty grasping the idea that such a loving, awesome, and all-wise God who did not spare His own Son, but gave Him up to suffer and die in such a cruel manner for even those who are in rebellion against Him would be impressed with just the mere physical death of man to the point of referencing it as being "precious in His sight"! That to me paints God in such a shallow and superficial light. I can, however, more accept that what is "precious in His sight" is the death of the self-life within, thereby allowing God to fill us and freely use us for His glory (**right here in this realm**), as I am more and more persuaded that **we are spiritually effective only to the degree to which we are surrendered to God**, and that requires the daily dying to self which surely impresses the Most High God!

Generally speaking, we seem to have far too much of a tendency to gauge spiritual effectiveness based on the level of activity a person is involved in, and further, how charismatic they may be in performing those activities. There is great danger in allowing oneself to become involved in a plethora of works to the point of allowing them to become the main focus and measurement of spiritual development, with little to no focus on actually dealing with the flesh. The Spirit of God knows the difference, and if we are spiritually sensitive enough He is able to show us clearly what the difference is (relationship with, and being led by the Spirit is the key).

> Matthew 7:21-23(NIV) – "Not everyone who says to me. 'Lord, Lord' will enter the Kingdom of heaven, but only he who does the will of my Father who is in

heaven. Many will say to me on that day (when I judge them), 'Lord, Lord, have we not prophesied in your name, and driven out demons in your name, and done many miracles in your name?' Then I will tell them plainly, 'I never knew you. Away from me, you evil doers!'"

"Does the Lord delight in burnt offerings and sacrifices as much as in obeying the Lord? To obey is better than sacrifice, and to heed is better than the fat of rams" – 1 Samuel 15:22(NIV)

New Creations

2 Cor 5:16-18(NIV) – "**So from now on we regard no one from a worldly point of view, though we once regarded Christ in this way we do so no longer. Therefore if anyone is in Christ, the new creation has come. The old has gone, the new is here.** All this is from God, who reconciled us to himself through Christ and gave us the ministry of reconciliation."

Judging from a worldly point of view (that is to say "after the flesh") is where we end up going down the wrong path, all the while leaning on our own understanding which God has warned us against doing. The Trinity is Spirit, we cannot relate to God through flesh-driven works; indeed, His ways are hidden from those who seek Him in the energy of the flesh! We need to "regard no one from a worldly point of view" **beginning first and foremost with our own individual selves**!

Years ago my wife and I attended a series of meetings at a church which were led by a couple of evangelists. There were nightly meetings conducted for the duration of seven days. I found the sessions I was able to attend to be very informative. There was a meeting scheduled for the following Saturday, which was designated as a time for testimonies. I was very interested in attending that one for sure. There was much sharing, and inspiring testimonies were presented. One lady volunteered to testify and she began by saying that she was very grateful for the blood of Jesus (choruses of "amen" were heard for sure!). However, she then went on to say "but" (immediately my spiritual antenna went higher!). She then went on to explain that her gratitude for the blood of Jesus was impacted by what she felt as a result of the scope of the sins she had to deal with in her life. She said that, as a result, she felt like a door that has had a hole knocked through it which had been fixed up and painted over. And that consequently she could never feel like a "new creation," but would always feel like a door that has a hole in it. I thank God to this day that my spirit was sensitive enough at that stage of my growth to hear Holy Spirit immediately inform me that I was not to receive that falsehood! The leaders of the meeting in response turned to the congregation and said, "You see, folks, that is the impact of sin". Which, while carrying a measure of truth, didn't fully address that which was at issue. Unfortunately, there were many "more seasoned Christians" (than myself) in attendance who emphatically responded "amen".

The sadness of that moment was that this lady, and those who agreed with her words, were (are) taken captive by the enemy's lies by denying the power of the blood of Jesus. Thank God for the truth of Isaiah 1:18(NIV) – "Come now, let us settle the matter" says the Lord. "Though your sins are like scarlet they shall be as white as snow; though they are red as crimson, they shall be as wool." This word and others, such as 2 Cor 5:17(NIV) – "Therefore if anyone is in Christ, the new creation has come: The old has gone, the new is here!" more than solidify the absolute ability of the blood of Jesus to completely deal with sin.

Also, in the words of the song writer (William Cowper), "There is a fountain filled with blood, drawn from Immanuel's veins; and sinners plunged beneath that flood lose <u>ALL</u> their guilty stains"!

To receive otherwise is to blatantly deny the unmistakable power of the blood of Jesus and to choose instead to ascribe a measure of truth to the enemy's lies and subsequently walk under a cloud of guilt rather than in the total freedom offered by a loving and merciful Father through the blood of his Son. John 8:36(NIV) – "So if the Son sets you free, you will be free indeed."

"My sin, Oh the bliss of this glorious thought; my sin, **not in part, but the whole**, is nailed to the cross, **and I bear it no more**; praise the Lord, praise the Lord, O my soul" ("It is Well With My Soul" by Horatio Spafford)

Furthermore, we must constantly reflect on the fact that the child of God is mandated to remain in a perpetual state of holiness so that relationship with God the Father (in fact with the Trinity) can become and remain an actuality. **To do so we have no choice but to rely on the sufficiency of His marvelous grace and walk in the consciousness that He (in His great wisdom and mercy) has not given us over to our own devices in order to attain such a lofty goal!**

> 1 Peter 1:13-16(NIV) – "Therefore with minds that are alert and fully sober, set your hope on the grace to be brought to you when Christ Jesus is revealed at his coming. As obedient children, do not conform to the evil desires you had when you lived in ignorance. But just as he who called you is holy, **so be holy in all you do; for it is written: 'Be holy, because I am holy'.**"

> 2 Peter 1:3(NIV) – "**His divine power has given us everything we need for a godly life** through our knowledge of him who called us by his own glory and goodness." Father understands the magnitude

of the struggles involved, that's why he has provided his marvelous grace, mercy, longsuffering, love and promises the likes of which include: 1 John 1:9(NIV) – "If we confess our sins, He is faithful and just to forgive us our sins, and to cleanse us from all unrighteousness; also Gal 5:16(NIV) – "So I say, walk by the Spirit and you will not gratify the desires of the flesh.

Foundational to this demand of holy living is that **we do not lean on our own understanding in determining whether we are individually meeting God's expectations**, but totally rely on the guidance and teaching of Holy Spirit. And to also recognize how the process can be greatly hindered (even nullified) if we are locked into a mentality of being "a door with a hole in it that has been fixed up and painted over". The path to holy living is hugely impacted and, subsequently, any hope of true fellowship with God, which is why those who are in such a "state" are in need of deliverance. 2 Cor 5:17(NIV) – **"Therefore if anyone is in Christ, the new creation has come: The old has gone, the new is here!"**

1 John 1:1-7(amplified bible) – "This is the message (of God's promised revelation) which we have heard from him and now announce to you, that God is light (he is holy, his message is truthful, he is perfect in righteousness), and in him there is no darkness at all (no sin, no wickedness, **no imperfection**). If we say that we have fellowship yet walk in darkness (of sin), we lie and do not practice the truth; but if we (really) walk in the light (**that is live each and every day in conformity with the precepts of God**) as he himself

is in the light, we have (true unbroken) fellowship with one another (he with us and we with him), **and the blood of Jesus His Son cleanses us from all sin (by erasing the stain of sin, keeping us cleansed from sin in all of its forms and manifestations)."**

The blood of Jesus is alive and active!

This matter of being "in Christ" is surely to be considered the greatest privilege ever proffered to man! Recognize, however, that in Him there is no sin, no wickedness, no imperfection (**no doors with holes that have been fixed up and painted over**), but rather "new creations"! God has made a way (through the blood of Jesus) for us to freely accept such an unspeakable, unimaginable, wondrous privilege, **not on our terms, but solely on His terms alone**!

Recognize also that God does not request that we do impossible things (those He takes care of). Hence, if He promises His children the awesome privilege of having unbroken fellowship with Him, He has made a way for it to happen: **live each and every day in conformity with the precepts of God.** (Gal 5:16(NIV) – "So, I say, walk by the Spirit and you will not gratify the desires of the flesh"). Indeed, if we are to comprehend the depth and value of such a privilege – "unbroken fellowship with God" - we must "think well" of God to the extent of realising that ABSOLUTELY NOTHING that this world has to offer could ever compare! Psalm 42:1 NIV) – "As the deer pants for streams of water, so my soul pants for you my God".

The pathway to this "unbroken fellowship", however, begins with surrender! Psalm 119 bountifully addresses the value of the precepts of God and the benefits of adhering to them. Additionally we need to seek clarification and understanding of the "precepts of God" as they pertain to our own individual lives. Although there is much commonality, we dare not pattern our walk solely based on what we see others doing. Neither should we try to live by the faith of another! Phil 2:12(NIV) – "…work out your salvation with fear and trembling!"

> Romans 1:17(NIV) – "For in the gospel the righteousness of God is revealed – a righteousness that is by faith from first to last, just as it is written: "**The righteous will live by faith**".
>
> (Hebrews 10:38(NIV) – "But my righteous one will live by faith. And I take no pleasure in the one who shrinks back")

There are moments when we all really need to pause and ask ourselves if we really do believe God's word (i.e. are we true believers?) I challenge myself regularly in that regard!

> 1 Cor 10:12(NIV) – "So, if you think you are standing firm, be careful that you don't fall."

Viewing the flesh as God's enemy

Unfortunately, many times we have heard of (or witnessed) a brother or sister experience a fall, occurring quite frequently after having risen through the "spiritual ranks"; mainly due to something related to the "works of the flesh"(there is the potential for it to happen to any of us). Further, when such things do happen we overlook, ignore, or minimize the actual impact on us, the body of Christ who are one (no matter where in the world "the fall" occurred)! The Word of God states that "the wages of sin is death!" We can no more ignore such "death" (whether it is physical, spiritual, or ministry- related) any more than we would ignore information from a medical specialist that a part of our own individual body has died or is dying. We need to weigh our reaction to such with these things in mind and also remind ourselves that "there, but for the grace of God go I" (Holy Spirit being our guide, lest we lean on our own understanding). Jer 17:9-10(KJ) – "The heart is deceitful above all things, and desperately wicked: who can know it? I the Lord search the heart and examine the mind, to reward each person according to their conduct, according to what their deeds deserve."

We dare not stand in judgement of others! Matthew 7:4-5(NIV) – "How can you say to your brother 'let me take the speck out of your eye', when all the time there is a plank in your own eye? You hypocrite, first take the plank out of your own eye, and then you will see clearly to remove the speck from your brother's eye."

Upon hearing about the fall of a dear brother in Christ, I was impacted to such an extent that I earnestly sought the Lord about how I personally can (better) do my part to prevent such a thing from happening to me. I should qualify this level of interest by highlighting the concern (indeed fear) I have about "the wages of sin being death", especially in light of the fact that God is not superficial, nor does He speak empty words, and not one of us is exempt from the possibility of falling! When one experiences a "fall", it's not a matter of just "getting up and dusting oneself off and moving on"; there is death of some dimension involved and what that pertains to is totally in God's hands, not ours. We have to look to Him for clarification of any steps toward restoration and not lean on our own understanding (nor the understanding of others!) Upon reflection of this, I often think, for instance, of what Samson experienced (Judges 13-16) in that, while God did restore his strength, and he was able to avenge himself, he had been rendered blind, having had his eyes gouged out by his enemies. God did not intend for that to happen to Samson, but he had made choices and the "wages" was the loss of his eyesight! Prior to this event we are told that Samson had become spiritually insensitive, to the degree that he did not know that the Lord had left him (Judges 16:20(NIV) – "Then she called, "Samson, the Philistines are upon you!" He awoke from his sleep and thought, "I'll go out as before and shake myself free." But he did not know that the Lord had left him.") **Yes, the Lord has promised "never to leave us nor forsake us". However, we must never allow ourselves to be deceived into thinking that he will dwell in peace in an unclean vessel!**

One time, in a moment of sweet fellowship, the Lord said to me, "I have need of you, but never entertain the thought that I can't do without you". A very sobering moment indeed!

Father's response to my question was that it very much depends on our attitude towards the flesh (His enemy). He then directed me to read Psalm 139:21-24(NIV). David declares, "Do I not hate those who hate you, Lord, and abhor those who rise up against you? I have nothing but hatred for them; I count them my enemies". David then goes on to ask God to search his heart (vs 23-24)! Father also directed me to Psalm 101(NIV) with a focus on verse 8. Here David declares, "Every morning I will put to silence all the wicked in the land; I will cut off every evil doer from the city of the Lord."

My request to God is that He make me aware of any flesh in me that I do not have such an attitude of hatred toward as I endeavor to daily effect its crucifixion in my own life!

Viewing the flesh as anything less than a treacherous enemy is foolhardy on our part, given that we are told that it desires what is contrary to the Spirit and the Spirit what is contrary to the flesh; **they are in constant conflict with each other** (thereby greatly impairing our ability to do the things we want to do – Gal 5:17)! An even more concerning issue is the impact which that has on our establishing and maintaining relationship with Jesus through Holy Spirit, and potentially jeopardizing our chances of being selected as the Bride of Christ Jesus which will definitely not be adorned by flesh. That should greatly alarm us!

Surely, if we claim to love the Lord our God whole-heartedly, being militant towards His enemies must become and remain the norm!

Matthew 11:12(KJ) – "From the days of John the Baptist until now, the Kingdom of heaven suffereth violence, and the violent take it by force." (The flesh wars against the Spirit and the Spirit against the flesh.)

I once read a suggestion that we deal with the flesh "ruthlessly, pitilessly, and permanently". The seriousness of its impact can never be overstated! I also often reflect on what Paul states in Romans 10:1-3(NIV) – "Brethren, my heart's desire and prayer to God for Israel is that they might be saved. For I can testify about them that they are zealous for God, but their zeal is not based on knowledge. Since they did not know the righteousness of God and sought to establish their own, they did not submit to God's righteousness."

Also in this regard I am reminded of the words of the songwriter Edward Mote : "When Christ shall come, with trumpet sound, Oh may I then in Him be found, **dressed in His righteousness alone**, faultless to stand before the throne". Let us be (and stay) reminded that God refers to our righteousness as "filthy rags" (Isaiah 64:6). Our being "well intentioned" in our acts of righteousness mean absolutely nothing if they are flesh-directed as opposed to Spirit-directed!

On waiting

God is completely void of any and all anxiety at all times, and our anxiety does not in any way dictate the speed of His response to our prayers or how He will answer! His direction to "tarry" may cause us varying levels of anxiety, worry, questioning, etc., but He is a God who is at peace at all times and he expects us to be the same; (He who says "the just shall live by faith")! The waiting is never easy, which is why He also said "Trust in the Lord with all your heart and lean not on your own understanding" (Proverbs 3:5(NIV)); also, "for my thoughts are not your thoughts, neither are your ways my ways" Isaiah 55:8(NIV)).

The danger (significantly so) is in our running ahead of Him due to our impatience and/or the impatience or misunderstanding of those who feel they know best, and who it may be important for us to placate.

The Lord once chastised me in a Tim Hortons drive-thru on my way to work one morning. I was running a bit late, and I should also add that the line was moving reasonably well. However, I felt a spirit of impatience starting to rise within me and I immediately heard His voice say: "Get rid of that!" The tone was such that it left no mystery about the level of seriousness involved. I dealt with that spirit immediately and also immediately found myself once again engaged in God's peace. He then went on to say, "I am a God who is at peace at all times and I expect the same of my children". I certainly remain very thankful for that teaching (and preparation) moment. It is so easy for us to make light of the fact that we are expected to "live, move, and have our being in Christ" (Acts 17:28 (NIV)). A place that only Holy Spirit can help us to arrive and remain at and be able to comprehend the implications of doing so—things which cannot be learned from the lips of man!

This is a good point at which to be reminded of examples of some of our brethren who experienced significant "wait times":

- Moses in the desert 40 years before God said he was ready to deliver His message to Pharaoh – "Let my people go!"
- Joseph languishing in prison for years while God showed him favor all the while, until the appointed time of his release to become second in command to Pharaoh
- David anointed as king, yet spending significant time running for his life before he got to sit on the throne of Israel

It is God's work which He accomplishes through yielded and surrendered vessels by the direction of His Spirit!

Holy Spirit alone knows what works God has assigned to us individually, and He alone knows at what stage of our individual crucifixion process we are ready to undertake the assigned labor.

How often have we sat and listened to some truly inspiring messages or teachings and felt like we were ready to conquer the world? The dust settles, and more and more the realization that we are not prepared for the journey dawns on us. Aside from the fact that those could be moments when God is wanting to stretch our faith in a particular area(s), more often than not we, in those moments, are not realizing the part that the flesh plays in absolutely keeping us from, or at the very least hampering progress towards fulfilling the purposes of God in our lives.

A major point which needs to be highlighted is the fact that, while God is more than able to do great and marvelous things in, and subsequently through, our individual lives, **we must have an attitude of surrender to Him** in order for those things to come to fruition, according to His plans and purposes! We can so get caught up in "naming and claiming" promises, and end up becoming discouraged and frustrated when we don't experience the wonderful things we heard presented via some sermon, teaching, bible study, time of sharing, etc. Proverbs 3:5-7(NIV) – "Trust in the Lord with all your heart and lean not on your own understanding; in all your ways submit to him, and he will make your paths straight. Do not be wise in your own eyes; fear the Lord and shun evil".

We also must recognize that the enemy actually uses the flesh as a weapon against us and subsequently against God! The enemy knows very well what "flesh buttons" to push! Hence it is wisdom to employ (as God pointed out to me) the attitude that David expresses in Psalms 139 and Psalms 101, expressing and employing a loathing (even perfect hatred) towards those who rise up against God and referring to them as his enemies (Psalm 139:21-22). In Psalms 101:8, David commits to daily taking strides to eliminate every evil doer from the "city of the Lord". Nothing short of crucifixion will solve the issue! Thank God for His grace, mercy, patience, longsuffering compassion, and love as we daily endeavor to take up our individual cross and follow the leading of Holy Spirit!

Further, if God is willing to be patient with us, it behooves us to learn not to beat ourselves up or allow despair or discouragement to linger in those moments when we blow it (and we sometimes will), as long as we acknowledge and confess our failings to Him (as Holy Spirit reveals them), then repent and trust in His forgiveness and restoration. I recall one occasion after I had blown it and began to berate myself for having done so, even to the point of questioning the Lord's decision for even placing a call on my life. His rebuke was immediate and firm in pointing out how audacious it was of me to question His decision making! While the rebuke was sharp, it did cause me to seek forgiveness for such folly; His subsequent words of enlightenment and encouragement brought much needed comfort. We overlook the fact that God does not choose us because we are perfect. And though He has promised to forgive and cleanse us from all unrighteous, if we acknowledge and confess our sins (1 John 1:9(NIV)), it does not constitute a license to sin. Our focus must be on the wonders that the Lord can perform through yielded and sanctified vessels, and not on our capability in the flesh! Father is more than aware that this matter of crucifying the flesh is so much more than an overnight journey ("Take up your cross daily.") He of course has not left us to our own accord to accomplish such a feat, He who has declared "Apart from me you can do nothing." Holy Spirit is always available to guide, teach, comfort, and counsel (and more). His "classroom" is always open! This is a good place to strongly suggest reading, studying, and digesting the fullness, (by the Spirit), of Psalms 139.

A further point to consider is that, while God loves His children far beyond what our limited understanding allows us to grasp, like any wise general He will never empower his enemy (the flesh within)! **Think of what a loss cause it becomes therefore, when**

we seek to be empowered by God yet ignore His instruction to surrender and crucify the flesh within.

> **Gal 5:24(NIV) – "Those who belong to Christ Jesus have crucified the flesh with its passions and desires."**

Just striving to be "good people" is not what we have been called to; otherwise, Christ Jesus suffered greatly and died in vain.

In the words of the song writer Rick Founds: "Lord we lift Your name on high"; "He came from heaven to earth to show the way…"

> Romans 8:8(KJ) – "So then they that are in the flesh cannot please God."

As the Lord continued to give me more and more understanding of how imperative it is for us to constantly and consistently deal with the flesh, I found myself earnestly praying that Holy Spirit would help me in that regard.

I am led at this point to share an experience I had at a weekend retreat many years ago. It started on a Friday evening at which point we were requested to retire early, as it was expected that we rise up early enough to be out of the building by 6am. The objective being to go for a walk and see if God had a word for us individually.

I left the building in the company of a few people who were chatting and joking. Keeping the objective in mind, I drew back from the group. Father immediately asked me if I was willing to go in a different direction. I agreed and He instructed me to go to my left. We had been walking along a path and on both sides there was waist-high brush. I parted the brush with my hands and began to notice that I was on somewhat of a slope. By now it was starting to get brighter. I reached a point where I could clearly see that the ground was indeed slopped and below was a field. I stood looking over the field and Father told me to go down onto it.

I made my way down and started walking around and He told me to sit down in the dirt. I sat down, and He said, "Look around – what do you see?" I responded, "The field has been plowed". He said, "Look again and tell Me what you see." This time I scanned with more regard and responded that, while the field had been plowed, there remained many clumps of weeds, stubble, and stumps, etc.

Father then told me that the field represented my life thus far; still a lot of clumps, stubble, and stumps, etc. remain. He then asked me what I wanted to do about it. I confess that my first thought was what the cost would be. Mind you, not just the cost, but also of being very conscious of words spoken or promises made to God! Deuteronomy 23:21-23(NIV) – "If you make a vow to the Lord your God, do not be slow to pay it, for the Lord your God will certainly demand it of you and you will be guilty of sin. But if you refrain from making a vow you will not be guilty. Whatever your lips utter you must be sure to do because you made your vow freely to the Lord your God with your own mouth."

In response to his question I simply replied, "They don't belong!" He then said to me, "That's true, but what do you want to do about it?" I found myself getting a bit flustered because I knew that He was not going to let go of it, and I was still not ready to commit. I then replied, "Father, we both know that they don't belong." He then, in his loving, compassionate, patient, understanding way, responded, **<u>"That is true, but</u> <u>what do you want ME to do</u>**

about it?" (Placing the emphasis on his willingness and ability to help me.) At that moment I began to reflect on the earnestness with which I had prayed and asked Him to help me to deal with the flesh according to His desires. I then responded, "I want You to remove them". He did not speak another word. I sat in the dirt for quite a while longer, pondering the "cost" of my commitment while also reflecting on the truth that God has been so good and faithful to me and mine, and that He has continually taken me deeper in understanding the depth of His love. Holy Spirit also reminded me of a word of encouragement that I had once read in a copy of a Daily Bread booklet, which reminded the reader, "Always remember that the pruning knife is in the hands of a loving Father". These thoughts brought much-needed comfort!

I returned to join the others, but I did not share my experience with anyone. I was trying to come to grips with it for myself.

Weeks passed, and more and more I began to feel an excruciating discomfort in my spirit. I would not have been able to describe the level of pain to anyone; indeed, it felt beyond description! In my mind I felt like I was being held in a vise and I was being "gouged" very deeply, and it hurt deep within my entire being! I equated the "gouging" to the act of removing some rot when peeling a fruit or vegetable. I am very acquainted with severe pain, as I have experienced a couple of vehicle accidents that caused me to have back pain which at times has prevented me from sitting, standing, or even walking. This was a pain, however, that was on another level. It made me want to run away (far), but I felt the vise-like grip!

This spiritual discomfort continued for what seemed like forever. So much so that, one evening, I cried out to Father, "Please help me, I feel like You have me in a vise and it feels like You are gouging me and I can't take it anymore, please stop it, please!"

Father responded, "You are like a little child who is trying to squirm out of its mother's arms, not understanding the place of safety that it is in. I want you to rest, it is only for a season". It was a comfort to hear Father's voice, as always. However, the gouging did not lessen and therefore neither did the discomfort, which was constant!

At the time I was enrolled in some theology courses. During the last evening of one of them, the instructor, whom I had never seen or heard of before, stated that he had a prophetic ministry and that if anyone cared to find out whether or not God had a word for them, he was willing to stay after class and pray with them. My immediate response (within myself) was that I did not want to hear any more words (as the gouging continued). I was going home! When I went to retrieve my coat, Holy Spirit said clearly, "I want you to stay and go to him." I was tired physically and I truly did not want to hear anything else.

One thing I have come to view more and more as a blessing is that, from my youth, I have always been prone to be very obedient. I heard Holy Spirit express His desire that I stay back and visit with this brother. The battle began, as I was very reluctant to hear anything else coupled with the fact that I am super reluctant to deliberately allow anyone to speak words over me. On occasion when it has happened, the word spoken has always been confirmation of what the Lord has already spoken to me. My tiredness, reluctance, and the discomfort from the "gouging" resulted in my being disobedient. When I finally made the decision to be obedient, I looked up and eight people had lined up to "hear a word", and there were others seemingly moving in that direction. If I had moved when Holy Spirit had prompted me I would have been first or second in line. My disobedience had cost me. (As it always does!)

I joined the line and listened intently as words were spoken and acknowledged.

When my turn came, this brother put his hands on each of my shoulders, bowed his head, and began by saying, "I see that the Lord has you in a vise" (Boy did he have my attention!). He then went on to say, "I also see that the Lord is chipping", then came a significant pause, and he continued, "No, it is not chipping, I would say that it is more like He is "gouging" you. And it appears that if you had your way you would squirm out of that place. The Lord is saying that He wants you to rest; He says it is only for a season, and at the end of that time He says He promises to turn you around and show you what He had to do. But for now He wants you to rest". **Confirmation!**

I was certainly mesmerized by the experience, but I remember having difficulty digesting it all. I went home and locked myself away with Father.

Over time, as the "gouging" lessened, more and more I found my relationship with the Lord to be on a different level (and growing). His "turning me around" to show me why He had to do the gouging (and what had to be gouged) continues to unfold through His increasing my understanding of His ways and precepts, as I choose to spend precious moments sitting at His feet (He has promised to be a rewarder of those who diligently seek Him – Hebrews 11:6-KJ). His work in me certainly continues along other lines, but I am definitely not sorry that the gouging has ended!

On another occasion, the Lord chose to deal with my flesh in "stealth mode". My wife and I were attending an evening church service. Towards the end of the service, the speaker stated that he felt sure that God wanted to pour out a blessing in our midst. The congregation responded gleefully of course. Just as the speaker finished the statement, the Lord said to me, "The blessings will start when you run". I froze in terror! I have never been one with a penchant for the spotlight (yet from my youth the Lord has always pushed me to the front on various occasions). There were a great number of people present; couple that with my definitely not being a "runner", and sheer panic gripped me. God was dealing with pride in me (which I viewed as my being "reserved").

I begged the Lord to select someone else (i.e. the spirit of pride in me begged), but He simply stated again, "The blessings will start when you run". I then went into begging-overdrive, and again He repeated the same thing. I was in the midst of trying another approach when He stopped me with a very emphatic command: **RUN**! I immediately stepped out into the aisle, ran to the front of the church, then from one side to the other several times until He told me to go back to my seat. After the service ended, one of the elders who also viewed me as being *reserved* asked me why I ran. I responded, "Because I was told to". He nodded his head with an "uh-huh", smiled, and walked away. I, too, was smiling at that point.

On yet another occasion at an early stage of my spiritual growth, I awoke to find myself immersed in a great depth of despair and anguish over joblessness and other issues; so much so that I instantly cried out to the Lord for deliverance with tears flowing freely. The Lord's response to me was: "Sing". To which I replied, "Sing, Father? I can't even put two words together right now and You expect me to sing?" He responded with a verse from the song, "Come We That Love the Lord" (Isaac Watts), namely, "Let those refuse to sing who never knew our God, but children of the heavenly King will speak their joys abroad". He then went on to say, "Yes, I expect you to sing!" I was still unable to respond, and He began singing: "The longer I serve Him, the sweeter He grows; the more that I love Him more love He bestows... (Bill and Gloria Gaither)". I felt a bit perturbed that my pity party was being interrupted, but He ignored my protest and kept singing. I eventually joined in verbally, as I was definitely not in the singing mood. He persisted, and eventually I found myself making a feeble attempt to actually sing. My voice grew stronger and stronger until I realized that He had actually stopped singing and I was heartily singing that song on my own. My spirit had been delivered!

Each of God's children is different, and He will deal with each of us accordingly. These are just examples of some of the ways He has chosen to deal with this child of God.

The salient point here is that, while the Lord has appropriately demanded that we must crucify the flesh, He has not (as always) left the process open to be defined by man or left us to our own efforts alone to accomplish the task. He has made it clear that He will only validate that which we allow His Spirit to guide us through.

Romans 8:13(NIV) – "For if you live according to the flesh you will die; **but if by the Spirit** you put to death the misdeeds of the body, you will live".

Anything short of total surrender falls short of the Lord's expectation. 1 Cor 6:19-20(NIV) – "Do you not know that your bodies are the temples of the Holy Spirit, who is in you, whom you have received from God? You are not your own; you were bought at a price. Therefore honor God with your bodies."

He is patient and long-suffering in helping us to arrive at such a point, as we demonstrate diligence in applying ourselves to yielding to Holy Spirit in order for Him to enlighten us. However, recognize that (as a rule), as it is in the natural so it is in the spiritual. Arriving at a place of surrender requires a significant trust level. It is not possible to get there without having a healthy relationship with the Lord. Just as on the human level, we do not just meet someone and immediately "surrender" our hearts to them. It takes a depth of relationship!

On yielding the heart

When dealing with potential converts the question is often posed: "Would you like to give your heart to Jesus?" as opposed to "Would you like to invite Jesus into your heart?"! The difference is huge!

The "seasoned Christian" needs to challenge themselves individually the same – "Have you given your heart to Jesus (to do with it as He desires?)"

There are no doubt many who have faithfully attended church for years and have in some cases risen to various "ranks" in church circles, but have never completed the "transaction"! Make no mistake about it, surrender **is mandatory, not optional** if we would expect to truly function according to God's design for us individually—all the while being led by the Spirit of God! Surrender is indeed foundational to the faith of the child of God. Furthermore, surrender is essential in order for us to be able to acknowledge and submit to the sovereignty of God in our individual lives and not just acknowledging His being sovereign in a general sense (otherwise how can we individually call Him our Lord?)! Our minds have to be renewed so that Holy Spirit can help us to understand the wisdom and benefits of surrender as opposed to the worldly view with its negative connotations associated with it (only Holy Spirit —our teacher—can do that). That's not to say that God cannot still use us to some extent (after all, He did use a donkey to do His bidding at one point – Numbers 22), but He is not a shallow or superficial God. His level of expectation is high because He expects us to "live, move, and have our being in Christ" (Acts 17:28-NIV); and to also "Rejoice always, pray continually, give thanks in all circumstances, for this is God's will for you in Christ" (1 Thess. 5:16-18-NIV). "I can do all things through Christ, which strengtheneth me" (Phil 4:13-KJ). These things being truth, we cannot expect God to deny His power by authorizing any effort that will glorify the flesh (His enemy!). God does not share His glory!

The heart must be surrendered if it is to be brought to a point of being a suitable abode for the Most High, awesome, majestic God!

> Jer 17:9-10(KJ) – "The heart is deceitful above all things and desperately wicked: who can know it? I the Lord search the heart, I try the reins, even to give every man according to his ways, and according to the fruit of his doings. Consider also God's promise in Matthew 5:8(KJ) – "Blessed are the pure in heart, for they shall see God".

"Oh to grace how great a debtor, daily, I'm constrained to be; let thy goodness, like a fetter, bind my wandering heart to thee; prone to wander Lord I feel it, prone to leave the God I love; here's my heart Oh take and seal it, seal it for thy courts above" ("Come Thou Fount of Every Blessing" – Robert Robinson).

Again, God has not given us over to our own natural ability to arrive at His desired place for us (individually and subsequently, corporately). He has assigned his Spirit the task of preparing the Bride of Christ, and that cannot happen unless we reach the place of surrender (which is arrived at in tandem with the elimination of the flesh). The book of Esther reflects this process beautifully, when subsequent to Queen Vashti's disobedience to King Xerxes, she is deposed and the search for a new queen is enacted. The "candidates" were subjected to a major renewal over the period of twelve months in order to potentially be selected as the king's bride! In order for the process to be brought to fruition, the candidates had to totally surrender to the one (Hegai – the king's eunuch) whom the king had chosen to prepare them.

In the same manner, we must be totally surrendered to Holy Spirit, thereby allowing Him to have His way with us!

My own attitude of surrender has certainly not come easy. Yes, I was seeking God, praying, reading and studying the bible constantly, attending church, seeking teaching through Holy Spirit; rejoicing, praying to be used by God. However, this issue of surrender would always arise in my spirit; to the point where I had tremendous difficulty singing the likes of "All to Jesus I surrender" with any trace of sincerity, which significantly bothered me. I finally reached a point where I confessed to Father that I was aware that my "ALL" was not yet laid on the altar of sacrifice and that I wanted it to be. He told me that if I wanted it to be so, just commit to it by faith and He would "meet me" at my level of faith and work with me (what a God of mercy!) It is indeed very much a process. However, our cooperation plays a huge part in determining how long a process it will be, (we must always bear in mind that there are things that have to be worked through (much of which we won't understand), which require time to unfold; **as the Lord pointed out to me, there is not only a need for learning, but also the need to "unlearn" many things**).

Every human being benefits in some way from the goodness of God. Matthew 5:45(NIV) – "He causes his sun to rise on the evil and the good, and sends rain on the righteous and the unrighteous." However, in the words of the song, "Trust and Obey", by John Henry Sammis, – "But we never can prove the delights of his love, until all on the altar we lay; for the favor He shows and the joy He bestows, are for them who will trust and obey."

It is imperative that we make relationship with God a top priority, seriously cultivate it daily, cherish it, and guard it well as the precious commodity that it is! Above all we need to ask Holy Spirit to teach us how to reverence the Trinity, which is not something to be appropriately learned from the lips of man! A child born into a royal family has to be taught appropriate protocol. They are not born with the insight! How much more the need for the child of the most High to learn how to approach and remain in the presence of our awesome God! ("Tolerate nothing that dulls the perception of his presence" —"Come Away My Beloved"by Frances J. Roberts).

The church also must recognize and eschew hyperbole (e.g. speaking words which are void of any substance); the word of God is exact and sure and needs no "propping up". Hebrews 4:12(NIV) – "For the word of God is alive and active. Sharper than any double-edged sword, it penetrates even to dividing soul and spirit, joints and marrow; it judges the thoughts and attitudes of the heart." Referencing the word of God in a flippant manner is irreverent to begin with and only leads to superficiality, which can only result in a very low view of God and the things of God—a most serious matter! I agree wholeheartedly with the following words of A. W. Tozer (*The Knowledge of the Holy*): "Low views of God destroy the gospel for all who hold them. It is impossible to keep our moral practices sound and our inward attitudes right while our idea of God is erroneous or inadequate; if we ever think well it should be when we think of God".

I would once again reiterate my seriousness when it comes to saying things or making promises to Father! He honors transparency in His children (it's not like He doesn't already know our every thought and motive – Psalms 139:1-4-NIV). The "fabric" of relationship with Him is all the more beautiful, rich and strong when there is yielding and obedience involved. There is no other way! **Then we can know the joy of walking in the confidence of His love!**

I constantly thank God for patiently bringing me to the point of surrender, when I was able to freely say to Him (visualizing my heart in my hands being lifted up to Him): "Here is my heart, Lord. I give it to You to do with as You see fit"! He then said to me, "You have just won a great victory"! He has further explained to me (over time), that the transformation of the surrendered heart requires that it be made undivided, uncluttered (we have no idea what lurks therein) and cleansed before it can be made a suitable dwelling for His presence alone, thereby greatly enhancing the possibility of it remaining focused and fixed – trusting in him (Psalms 112:7-8-NIV). In this regard I have personalized a prayer request that David made in Psalms 86:11(NIV): "Teach me your way, Lord, that I may rely on your faithfulness; **give me an undivided heart that I may fear your name**". Subsequent to making this decision I began to experience a greater level of His peace and a greater level of faith. Indeed, I count yielding my heart to my Lord as the greatest and wisest decision I have ever made!

Now I can say with much determination: "Prone to wander, Lord I feel it; Prone to leave the God I love; here's my heart oh take and seal it, seal it (with the Blood of Jesus) for thy courts above" ("Come Thou Fount of Every Blessing" by Christopher Rice).

I am convinced that this (surrender), in conjunction with faithfully walking in obedience to Holy Spirit and "taking up one's cross daily" comprises the "narrow way" which He references in Matthew 7:13-14(NIV) – "Enter through the narrow gate. For wide is the gate and broad is the road that leads to destruction, **and many enter through it**. But small is the gate and narrow the road that leads to life, **and only a few find it.**"

I find those words "and only a few find it" to be among the most chilling! I neither wish to explore or even comprehend what it means to enter through the "wide gate". I long to be one of the "few"; that is my aim, my focus, and my strong desire! We are not our own, but have been bought with a price—the priceless blood of Jesus! **We don't get to choose how we are going to satisfy God**! Father does not speak empty words (and neither will His words return to Him void – Isaiah 55:11)!

Something else to ensure that we truly come to grips with, in regards to "not being our own", is the fact that Holy Spirit has not been placed within us solely as a "guest of the soul". Rather, He has come to take complete control; the onus of surrender is our responsibility! It won't be forced on us, we have to choose! Romans 8:14(NIV) – "For those who are led by the Spirit of God are the children of God."

Then, once having been given control, Holy Spirit is able to appropriately fulfill His mandate including (to highlight a few): leading us in paths of righteousness – Psalms 23:3(KJ); teaching us – 1 John 2:27(NIV) – "As for you, the anointing you received from Him remains in you, **and you do not need anyone to teach you**. But as His anointing teaches you about all things and as that anointing is real, not counterfeit—just as it has taught you, remain in Him."; aiding us in the renewal of our minds – Romans 12:2(NIV) – "Do not conform to the pattern of this world, but be transformed by the renewing of your mind. Then you will be able to test and approve what God's will is—his good, pleasing, and perfect will."

Such mandate cannot be effected appropriately with the flesh being completely free to be in constant conflict with the Spirit! The intensity of the conflict will lessen more and more as we continually crucify (deny) the flesh.

The objective being to strive for the moment when we can sing the likes of the words expressed by the Bill and Gloria Gaither: "It is finished, the battle is over; it is finished, there will be no more war; it is finished, the end of the conflict; it is finished, **and Jesus is Lord.**"

"The end of the conflict" is of course that place of total surrender—which is realised in stages. Father will never give us more than we can bear (in the spirit), so the "stages" which come in the form of tests and trials are designed to solidify our maturation in Christ. We don't get to move from stage to stage without passing the designated test(s)! Should we fail a test, He will allow it again in a different manner. In that way He ensures that the substance of our faith is firm. As faith increases we begin to have a better understanding of their necessity and purpose (just as in our earthly school days). I remember saying to Father at a very early stage of my spiritual growth that I could never see myself expressing the words of the song "Through it All"(Andrae Crouch) – ("I thank him for the mountains and I thank him for the valleys, and I thank him for the storms he brought me through…"). Sometime, much later (after many tests and trials), I was in a place of rest and it suddenly dawned on me that I was indeed not just singing that song, but with much expression. It caused me to laugh heartily as Holy Spirit reminded me of the words I had spoken (with much conviction) to Father about thinking that I could never see myself expressing such sentiment; and I know that Father was laughing with me!

As previously mentioned, a scripture which God gave me at a very early stage of my growth is Isaiah 7:9(NIV) – "If you do not stand firm in your faith, you will not stand at all"; which came at a time when I was dreading the very thought of any tests. God is so good!

Christ Jesus is now spirit, He is no longer in the flesh; and further, according to Acts 17:28(NIV) – "For in Him we live move and have our being" (as brand new spirit creations)! Thereby making it imperative (at the very least) that the words of our mouth and the mediations of our hearts be always acceptable to God! Indeed, the only way we can find ourselves in such a glorious destination is through unwavering obedience to Holy Spirit, through our faith, and through the renewal of our minds (Romans 12:2(NIV) – "do not conform to the pattern of this world, but be transformed by the renewing of your mind").

Unless we constantly remind ourselves that God is not superficial in nature (in an extreme sense), and remain in the habit of constantly looking to God to check our "spiritual alignment" using His "plumb-line", and to also pinpoint any "spiritual leakage" (which can result if we do not guard our hearts with all diligence!), we are always in danger of getting out of synch with Him. He will give us wisdom if we ask (as He has promised James 1:5). However, He never intends for us to go off on our own, accomplishing things without Him, which is the dangerous and fruitless path of those who have their minds set on "bigging up" themselves rather than on glorifying God!

On being viewed as being fanatical

I have heard individual speakers state that one does not have to be a "fanatic" with regards to Christianity. I have never gotten to ask any of them to define what being a fanatic means from their perspective, but I have so much wanted to do so. The dictionary defines fanatical as being filled with excessive and single-minded zeal. My spirit cringes whenever I hear such advice being given because, to begin with, if the average Christian would be honest, the thought of pursuing God in a "fanatical" manner is extremely far from their norm anyway! In response to such advice I would simply point out what God has to say about seeking Him and finding Him:

- Numbers 32:1(NIV) – "Because they have not followed me **<u>wholeheartedly</u>**, not one of those who were twenty years old or more when they came up out of Egypt will see the land I promised on oath to Abraham, Isaac, and Jacob."
- Deuteronomy 6:4-5(NIV) – "Hear, O Israel: The Lord our God is one. Love the Lord your God with all your heart and with all your soul and with all your strength. These commands that I give to you today are to be on your hearts. Impress them on your children. Talk about them when you sit at home and when you walk along the road, when you lie down and when you get up. Tie them as symbols on your hands and bind them on your foreheads. Write them on the doorframes of your houses and on your gates."

- Jeremiah 29:13(NIV) – "You will seek me and find me when you **seek me with all you heart.**"
- Matthew 5:6(NIV) – "Blessed are those who **hunger and thirst** for righteousness, for they shall be filled."
- Matthew 22:37(NIV) – "Jesus replied 'Love the Lord your God **with all your heart** and **with all your soul** and **with all your mind,**'"
- Hebrews 11:6(KJ) – "But without faith it is impossible to please Him, for he that cometh to God must believe that he is, **and that he is a rewarder of them that diligently seek him,**"
- James 4:8(NIV) – "**Come near to God** and he will come near to you. Wash your hands, you sinners, and purify your hearts, you double-minded."
- Rev 3:14-16(NIV) – "to the angel of the church in Laodicea write: These are the words of the Amen, the faithful and true witness, the ruler of God's creation. I know your deeds, that you are neither cold nor hot. I wish you were one or the other! So, because you are lukewarm – neither hot nor cold – I am about to spit you out of my mouth."

Exercising anything resembling a laid back, lackadaisical, nonchalant, uninspired, etc., approach to seeking God is not going to suffice as indicated by the above scripture references. We deal with multiple distractions from day to day (indeed, significantly more than even in recent years) hence, having what may amount to a "cursory" type of approach to seeking God will only lead to frustration and severe lack of fulfillment as pertains to establishing and cultivating relationship with Him. **We need Jesus now more than ever!** Let us be reminded that Jesus has advised us to "enter through the narrow gate" and he also said that only a few will find it (Matthew 7:13). A cursory approach to developing relationship with him will therefore definitely not suffice!

If seeking God whole-heartedly with a single-minded zeal makes me a "fanatic" in the eyes of some, I gladly declare **AMEN!**

On Becoming Part of the Trinity

Col 2:8-10(NIV) – "See to it that no one takes you captive through hollow and deceptive philosophy, which depends on human tradition and the elemental spiritual forces of this world rather than on Christ. For in Christ all the fullness of the deity lives in bodily form, **and in Christ you have been brought to fullness**. He is the head over every power and authority."

John 14:15-21(NIV) – "**If you love me keep my commands**, and I will ask the Father, and he will give you another advocate to help you and be with you forever – the Spirit of truth. The world cannot accept him, because it neither sees him nor knows him. But you know him **for he lives with you and will be in you**. I will not leave you as orphans; I will come to you. Before long, the world will not see me anymore, but you will see me. Because I live, you also will live. **On that day you will realize that I am in the Father, and you are in me, and I am in you**. Whoever has my commands and keeps them is the one who loves me. The one who loves me will be loved by my Father, and I too will love them and show myself to them."

("On that day" (**I believe suggests the day that we surrender to Holy Spirit – thereby allowing him to have his way in us**) "you will realize that **I am in the Father, you are in me, and I am in**

you") **Further in this regard we must ensure that we do not gloss over the fact that God measures our love for him by our obedience to him!**

> John 14:22-23(NIV) – "Then Judas (not Judas Iscariot) said. "But Lord, why do you intend to show yourself to us and not to the world?" Jesus replied, "Anyone who loves me will obey my teaching. My Father will love them, **and we will come to them and make our home with them.**

Hence the reality is that God's plan involves the inclusion of his children **as part of the Trinity**. The challenge of our accepting such a magnificent truth can only be achieved by allowing Holy Spirit to give us the understanding of the fullness of the implications and ramifications involved, and the journey begins with our measure of faith (even if it be the size of a mustard seed). **God does not deal in hyperbole** (which is why we need to reject it on all fronts); His word is solid! He has called us to live by faith, trusting in His Word with the understanding that it will never return to Him void!

> 3:1-3 – "Since then you have been raised with Christ, set you hearts on things above, where Christ is seated at the right hand of God. Set your minds on things above, not on earthly things. **For you died, and your life is now hidden with Christ in God**."

I am reminded of a song called "Deeper" (taught to me by my spiritual father): "Deeper in thy love, O Jesus, doth my spirit cry to go, until all my life is hidden deep within the cleansing flow" (Chorus) – "Deeper in that holy life, till I'm lost with Christ in

God; hidden with my blessed Lord, while I walk this earthly sod" (L. C. Hail)

There are other verses, however I chose verse one (along with the chorus) as a focal point because it succinctly expresses the essence of what we are actually called to "in Christ"! Deeper in understanding and application – "**till we are lost with Christ in God; hidden with our blessed Lord, while we walk this earthly sod**"!

In him we are meant to "live, move and have our being"!

This is certainly not an overnight journey (to receive, accept, and make application of); and it is not a journey that will be forced on us (James 4:8 – "**Come near to God and He will come near to you…**" also Jer 29:13 – "**You will seek me and find me when you seek me with your whole heart**"); although it is the desire of God's heart that we would choose it; **indeed even crave after it**! The onus is on the individual to show God that we mean business, and He will surely respond (Hebrews 11:6 – "**And without faith it is impossible to please God, because anyone who comes to him must believe that he exists, and that he rewards those who earnestly seek him**."! What greater designation is there than to become a part of the Triune God through His son Christ Jesus; only Holy Spirit can gives us the understanding of something so precious and priceless! (**I am in the Father, you are in me and I am in you.**)

The Apostle Paul issues a challenge for any who would call themselves "Christian". 2 Cor 13:5(NIV) – "Examine yourselves to see whether you are in the faith; test yourselves, **do you not realize that Christ Jesus is in you – unless of course, you fail the test**"?

Jesus said that we are able to know! (John 14:20)

> 1 John 2:3-6 – "We know that we have come to know him if we keep his commands. Whoever says, "I know him." But does not do what he commands is a liar, and

the truth is not in that person. But if anyone obeys his word, love for God is truly made complete in them. This is how we know we are in him: whoever claims to live in him must live as Jesus did." (NIV)

Surely, if we can find ourselves on the positive side of such a test, we shouldn't have to greatly stretch our faith in order to accept being a part of the Trinity—there is no room for denial—it is ordained by God (if we would profess to be in Christ)!

I would share an instruction that Holy Spirit gave me at one point: "**When God gives you a word just 'EAT IT' - do not give it over to the carnal mind to unravel – you will lose out**"- **the carnal mind of course being hostile toward God – Romans 8:7**) In His time God will provide understanding. Also, do not try to live by the faith of another, rather allow Holy Spirit to "grow" you! We are individually called to live and grow according to our own individual measure of faith!

This is also a good time to be reminded of Paul's prayer in Eph 1:15-23(NIV) – "For this reason, ever since I heard about your faith in the Lord Jesus and your love for all God's people, I have not stopped giving thanks for you, remembering you in my prayers. I keep asking that the God of our Lord Christ Jesus, the glorious Father, may give you the Spirit of wisdom and revelation, **so that you may know him better**. I **pray that the eyes of your heart may be enlightened in order that you may know the hope to which he has called you, the riches of his glorious inheritance in his holy people, and his incomparably great power for us who believe**. That power is the same as the mighty strength he exerted when he raised Christ from the dead and seated him at his right hand in the heavenly realms far above all rule and authority, power and dominion, and every name that is invoked, not only in the present age but also in the one to come; and God placed all things under his feet and appointed him to be head over everything for the church, which is his body, the fullness of him who fills everything in every way."

Walking in the mentality of being part of the Trinity through Christ Jesus (as does overcoming generally in the life of a Christian) primarily involves major warfare within the mind: Romans 12:2(NIV) – "Do not conform to the pattern of this world, but be transformed by the renewing of your mind. Then you will be able to test and approve what God's will is – his good, pleasing and perfect will."

In the absence of being able to address even a good measure (let alone the fullness) of what being made part of the Trinity involves, one point Holy Spirit has impressed upon me thus far (as a starting point) is how important it is for us to practice "knowing no one according to the flesh", **beginning first and foremost with our individual selves!** 2 Cor 5:16-17(NIV) – "So from now on we regard no one from a worldly point of view. Though we once regarded Christ in this way, we do so no longer. Therefore, if anyone is in Christ, the new creation has come. The old has gone, the new is here!"

As previously mentioned, it is imperative that we "think well" when it comes to God and the "things" of God! That we don't allow our carnal thinking to dictate how we approach and commune with the most High. Firstly, we are called to relate to Him in Spirit (no alternative)! We can very easily mistake the emotional (fleshliness), for spiritual! John 4:23(NIV) – "Yet a time is coming and has now come when the true worshipers will worship the Father in the Spirit and in truth, for they are the kind of worshipers the Father seeks".

Rather than trying to find our way into such a place, we must look to Holy Spirit to guide us and give us understanding in order to comprehend the scope of worship which is acceptable to God, which involves so much more than just "lifting up a song"; but rather embraces lifestyle, for which the bedrock must be obedience! "Trust and obey, for there is no other way"! Otherwise our worship is shallow at best! We can't get there without relationship; and through relationship, Holy Spirit, our guide and teacher, can direct us into "thinking well" of God.

Lest we forget, we need to constantly consider God's reminder to us in Isaiah 55:8-9(NIV) – "For my thoughts are not your thoughts, neither are your ways my ways, declares the Lord. As the heavens are higher than the earth, so are my ways higher than your ways and my thoughts than your thoughts." This should cause us to consider asking God for guidance constantly and to look for His seal of approval (even when the way seems clear). As my spiritual dad would say, "at every bend of the road". I remain grateful for such a friend (Dr. Alton Gould) whom God used as a "road sign" in my life—always pointing me to the Lord for understanding; thereby pressing me to seek God for myself as opposed to constantly impressing his views upon me. (Beware of those who would block your path to relationship with God by presenting themselves as your only access to him!)

I have also been given the understanding that it is imperative that we rid ourselves of the thought and expression, "I am only human". Recognize that the God who formed us in our mother's womb utterly and completely understands human nature! Yet, this God (who is wisdom) has called us to be a part of Himself through his Son; recognize also that the conditions of doing so are clearly defined by God alone as we gain understanding via His precepts! As mind-boggling as this sounds, we reject it at our own great loss and peril! "**Henceforth know ye no one according to the flesh.**"

My Proclamation

That which I am about to share is insight (which I refer to as my Proclamation) which Holy Spirit has opened up to me over a period of years (much of which I have already shared in this writing), as I have sat quietly and allowed Him to feed me! He has indeed had to uproot, re-establish, change, and eliminate, etc., many insights/habits that I had acquired during my journey thus far (and it continues to evolve). I continually speak these truths into the atmosphere. The Lord has promised to be a rewarder of those who diligently seek Him, and that has been and is my desire. His return is near and He is returning for a church that has more than just a form of godliness!

My prayer is that the reader will read and reflect on these truths (many times over) and ask Holy Spirit to provide His perspective to you personally, as only He can enlighten the individual as to the implications and ramifications of being made a part of the Trinity; we dare not lean on our own understanding (nor the understanding of others). There are many Scripture references, but it also includes some of which Father has spoken to me directly:

The fullness of God the Father is in Christ Jesus His son; the fullness of Christ Jesus is in God the Father.

The fullness of God the Father is in Holy Spirit; the fullness of Holy Spirit is in God the Father.

The fullness of Christ Jesus is in Holy Spirit; the fullness of Holy Spirit is in Christ Jesus.

All of the fullness of Holy Spirit has been placed within me by God the Father (John 14:7-11; John 14:16-24; John 17; John 15:26; John 16:5-15 - NIV).

Making me one in spirit with Christ Jesus, in whom I am meant to live, move, and have my being (Acts 17:28; Col 3:1-4 - NIV).

You said that you would not leave us comfortless, but that you would come to us; you said "if you love me (John 14:15 NIV), you will obey me, and I will ask the Father, who will send the Spirit of truth, who will be with you forever"! Indeed, you said that He will be "in us"! (John 7:37-39 NIV)

You said "on that day" (the day that we totally surrender to Holy Spirit, thereby allowing Him to have His way in us) we will know that you are in the Father, we are in you and you (by Holy Spirit) are in us! (John 14:16-26 NIV)

You also said "see to it that no one takes you captive, through hollow and deceptive philosophy, which comes by human tradition and the basic principles of this world, rather than through Christ; for in Christ Jesus all the fullness of the Deity dwells in bodily form, and in Christ you have been brought to fullness"; (and I thereby have received fullness of the Father; fullness of Jesus, and fullness of Holy Spirit through Christ Jesus); who has been given authority over **EVERY** principality and power(Col 2:8-10-NIV); and you have vested me with your authority so that I too (through Christ Jesus) also have authority over **EVERY** principality and power! (Eph 1:15-23-NIV)

Since you are in the Father, I am in you and you are in me, I can thereby boldly and confidently proclaim that I am being made part of the Trinity through Christ Jesus. Which is why you have said, "You must be holy because I am holy" (Lev 10:1-3; Lev

16:2; 1 Peter 1:13-16 - NIV)! You have not given us over to our own devices to attain such a lofty goal; but your divine power has given us **EVERYTHING** we need for life and godliness (2 Peter 1:3-8-NIV)! (Through our relationship with you, our understanding of your ways, and our obedience to your Spirit!) "You who have called us by your grace and mercy; and through these, you have given us your great and wonderful promises; so that through your promises, we can partake of the divine nature and escape the corruption of the world". One of the greatest of your promises, which is so little understood, and applied in our lives is, if we will walk in obedience to your Spirit, we will not gratify the desires of the sinful nature (Gal 5:16-NIV), and thereby be kept from falling so that we can be presented faultless before your throne, (clothed in your righteousness) as the Bride of Christ.

You have said "Whoever wants to be my disciple must deny themselves, take up their cross daily and follow me" (Luke 9:23-NIV)! You also said that "those who belong to Christ Jesus have crucified the flesh with its passions and desires" (Gal 5:24-NIV); and that "the Kingdom of heaven suffereth violence, and the violent take it by force (Matthew 11:12-KJ); "For the flesh desires what is contrary to the Spirit, and the Spirit what is contrary to the flesh. They are in conflict with each other, so that you are not to do whatever you want" (Gal 5:17-NIV).

I therefore declare as David did; "I hate those who hate you and loathe those who rise up against you; I have nothing but hatred for them, and I count them my enemies" (Psalm 139:21-22-NIV).

I also declare as David did – "morning after morning I will root out all the wicked (flesh) of the land (my being), that I may eliminate EVERY evil doer from the city of God" (Psalm 101:8-NIV).

Through acts of obedience which leads to righteousness, which in turn leads to holiness (Romans 6:16-19 - NIV), I am perfecting holiness out of reverence for the Trinity of which I am being made part of through Christ Jesus! (2 Cor 6:14-18, 7:1-NIV); always endeavoring to ensure that the words of my mouth and the meditations of my heart are acceptable to the Trinity; "for I have died (through the process of crucifixion of the flesh), and my life is now hidden with Christ, in God" (Col 3:3-NIV).

In Christ I am being made a brand new creation – the "old" with reference to the flesh is being crucified; the "new" with reference to the Spirit has come ; 2Cor 5:16-17(NIV) - "So from now on we regard no one from a worldly point of view. Though we once regarded Christ in this way we do so no longer. Therefore if anyone is in Christ the new creation has come: the old has gone, the new is here". (**It is imperative that we establish this mindset within ourselves first!**)

I am also being made the righteousness of God through Christ, which facilitates my being His ambassador; having been charged with the ministry of reconciliation (to reconcile others to God through Christ – 2Cor 5:18-NIV)

In my "position" in Christ Jesus - **(AS PART OF THE TRINITY)** – I can never be defeated "Thanks be to God who always causes me to triumph, through Christ Jesus; and He spreads through us throughout, the fragrance of the knowledge of Himself…….." (because from Father's perspective, the more I eliminate the flesh in me, He is **THEN** able to fill me), and I become more and more the aroma of His son, to those who are perishing and to those who are being saved; to one we are the smell of death; to the other, we are the fragrance of life! (2Cor 2:14-16-NIV)

God is light (He is holy, His message is truthful, He is perfect in righteousness), and in Him **there is no darkness at all (no sin, no wickedness, no imperfection); if we will walk <u>daily</u>** in conformity to His precepts, we are able to have unbroken fellowship with Him; and the Blood of Jesus cleanses us from all sin by erasing the stain of sin, keeping us cleansed from sin in all its forms and manifestations! (1 John 1:5-7 Amplified Bible).

Summation

We are spiritually effective only to the degree to which we are surrendered, it is otherwise bogus to label ourselves as being "Spirit filled" or "Spirit led" based solely on our works, charisma, faithful church attendance, etc.! God intends to perform His will through those who are led by Holy Spirit, which requires a constant looking to Him for guidance along with appropriate response. This very much implies relationship (lest on "that day" we would hear the Lord say "depart from me, I never knew you")! In plain language, the flesh is in the way of God's will being accomplished to His satisfaction; there is absolutely no allowance for "co-piloting"; Hence His command to crucify the flesh!

Gal 5:24(NIV) –"<u>Those who belong to Christ Jesus have crucified the flesh with its passions and desires.</u>"

Romans 8:5-9(NIV) – "Those who live according to the flesh have their minds set on what the flesh desires; but those who live in accordance with the Spirit have their minds set on what the Spirit desires. The mind governed by the flesh is death, but the mind governed by the Spirit is life and peace. The mind governed by the flesh is hostile to God; it does not submit to God's law, nor can it do so. **<u>Those who are in the realm of the flesh cannot please God.</u>**

I once heard an analogy along these lines: a parent instructs their child to go and brush his/her teeth, wash up, and put on their pajamas in preparation for bed time. The child disappears and returns to the room fully clothed (just as when he/she had departed), with a piece of paper in hand. The child announces to the parent, "Look at the beautiful picture I have drawn for you". The parent takes the paper and responds, "You are right, it certainly is a beautiful picture. However, I gave you specific instructions to brush your teeth, wash up, and put on your pajamas!"

God has provided specific instructions pertaining to many issues and provided specific directions on satisfying His demands! Developing and maintaining relationship with God is essential (in fact, crucial) in helping us to ensure that we avoid committing similar folly in terms of offering God "beautiful pictures" in lieu of obedience when He instructs us. The seriousness of such action can be seen (as a sample), in God's dealing with King Saul in 1 Samuel 15 (it cost Saul the Kingdom of Israel). 1 Samuel 15:22(NIV) – "But Samuel replied, "Does the Lord delight in burnt offerings and sacrifices as much as in obeying the voice of the Lord? To obey is better than sacrifice, and to heed is better than the fat of rams."

I am reminded of a time years ago, when I asked the Lord to help me to develop relationship with Him. I started off by devoting a specific time of just being still before Him. This went on for quite a long period of time, but I was determined to hear His voice. Finally one evening, I was kneeling at the time (God checks the heart more than the position of one's body), and after a significant period of time I determined that it probably was not going to happen on that occasion. I lifted one knee to rise up and I heard Him say, "Stay with Me a while longer". I don't have words to express the level of excitement that I felt. I did stay and He shared some things with me and intimacy was launched!

God has promised to be a rewarder of those who diligently seek Him, and if we do so, **in His time** He will never fail to keep His promises (He is a covenant-keeping God).

I share this to encourage any who would doubt the possibility of ever truly hearing from God. **Being surrendered to Him demands it!** To any doubters, I would simply pose the concept of communicating with any loved ones, especially those who have children of their own or are guardians: if you have something to communicate to your child (or anyone for that matter), is it your "preference" to ask someone to deliver the message for you, or is it your "preference" to go to your child or loved one and say "such and so"? I have determined in my heart to hear from God personally because I believe (indeed know!) that He is my heavenly Father who loves me far beyond my understanding, and I am fully persuaded that it is His "preference" to speak with me (indeed all of His children) **directly**; and I will not allow myself to be otherwise persuaded! We just have to show Him that we mean business! We also have to look to Him to help us to get past the apprehensions of what He might require of us. Some may prefer to have God's word for them passed on from someone thinking that it allows some "wiggle room", should it be something viewed as being too challenging. Developing intimacy with Him will serve to dispel such fears as one's trust level and confidence in him increases over time.

If the church is to truly function according to God's design (having more than just a form of godliness as a result), we must (at a minimum):

- individually surrender to (and obey) His Spirit, allowing Him to renew our minds. Thereby enabling us to "think well" of God and the things of God with the appropriate attitude and level of reverence as we receive revelation from him.
- recognize the futility of not being surrendered; and that surrender and obedience are not optional, if Christ Jesus is to be truly Lord of our lives.
- beware of statements of surrender made in ecstasy, lest they be retracted soon after (**in the face of trials and tests which must follow**).
- recognize the need to ask Holy Spirit to reveal any fears or apprehensions of surrendering for what they are (from God's perspective).
- avoid being locked in to "denominational thinking" so that true unity within the "Body of Christ" can manifest as the Spirit of God leads: Gal 3:26-29(NIV) – "So in Christ Jesus you are all children of God through faith, for all of you who were baptized into Christ have clothed yourselves with Christ. **There is neither Jew nor Gentile, neither slave or free, nor is there male or female, for you are all one in Christ Jesus.** If you belong to Christ, then you are Abraham's seed, and heirs according to the promise".
- recognize that we do not get to dictate the terms of relationship with God.

- focus on God's mandated priorities for our individual lives, e.g. (Romans 12:2(NIV) – "Do not conform to the pattern of this world, but be transformed by the renewing of your mind. Then you will be able to test and approve what God's will is – his good, pleasing and perfect will.")
- recognize how imperative it is to cultivate relationship with God daily; given that He has called us beyond simply just being faithful church attendees into personal relationship with Him through His Son with the teaching, guidance and help of His Holy Spirit.
- recognize and accept the fact that **we are not our own**, but have been bought with the blood of Jesus (and that Holy Spirit has the mandate of guiding us into paths of righteous living; we make the choice to follow Him or reject His leadership).
- recognize that it is impossible to be "in Christ" and not accept(by faith) being part of the Trinity ("in Him we live move and have our being").
- recognize that Jesus is now spirit (He is no longer in the flesh); hence "living, moving and having our being" in Him can only be in the spirit (**1 Cor 15:50(NIV)** – "I declare to you brothers and sisters, that flesh and blood cannot inherit the kingdom of God, nor does the perishable inherit the imperishable."). We have received a directive from Christ Jesus to focus on crucifying the flesh **daily** in order to facilitate our moving in the Spirit! **Romans 8:6-8(NIV)** – "The mind governed by the flesh is death, but the mind governed by the Spirit is life and peace. The mind governed by the flesh is hostile to God; it does not submit to God's law, nor can it do so. Those who are in the realm of the flesh

cannot please God." (Neither are they able to "live move and have their being in Christ Jesus"!)

- recognize that without faith it is **impossible** to please God (Heb 11:6)!
- recognize how crucial it is to avoid "leaning on our own understanding".
- take heed of the Lord's directive: "apart from me you can do nothing" (John 15:5-NIV)
- recognize the futility of trying to please God by just being "good church going folk" who are absorbed in activities which are not Spirit-directed (which lack any value in restraining sensual indulgence – Col 2:20-23 - NIV).

Hidden with Christ in God

Col 3:1-4(NIV) – "Since then you have been raised with Christ, set you hearts on things above, where Christ is seated at the right hand of God. Set your mind on things above, not on earthly things. **For you died and your life is now hidden with Christ in God.** When Christ, who is your life, appears, then you also will appear with him in glory".

Romans 8:9(NIV) – "You, however are not in the realm of the flesh but are in the realm of the Spirit, **if indeed the Spirit of God lives in you**. And if anyone does not have the Spirit of Christ, they do not belong to Christ."

John 14:19-23(NIV) - "Before long, the world will not see me anymore, but you will see me. Because I live, you also will live. **On that day, you will realize that I am in the Father, and you are in me, and I am in you**. Whoever has my commands and keeps them is the one who loves me. The one who loves me will be loved by my Father, and I too will love them and show myself to them. Then Judas (not Judas Iscariot) said, "But, Lord, why do you intend to show yourself to us and not to the world?" Jesus replied, anyone who loves me will obey my teaching. My Father will love them, and **we will come to them and make our home with them.**"

John 17:21(NIV) – "That they may be one, Father, just as you are in me and I am in you. May they also be in us so that the world may believe that you have sent me"

Col 1:24-27(NIV) – "Now I rejoice in what I am suffering for you, and I fill up in my flesh what is still lacking in regard to Christ's afflictions, for the sake of his body, which is the church. I have become its servant by the commission God gave me to present to you the word of God in its fullness – **the mystery that has been kept hidden for ages and generations, but is now disclosed to the Lord's people. To them God has chosen to make known among the gentiles the glorious_riches of this mystery, <u>which is Christ in you</u>, the hope of glory**.

2 Cor 13:5(NIV) – "Examine yourselves to see whether you are in the faith; test yourselves. <u>**Do you not realize that Christ Jesus is in you**</u> – unless of course, you fail the test?"

"Deeper in Thy love O Jesus, does my spirit cry to go; Until all my life is hidden, deep within that crimson flow; Deeper in that holy life, <u>**till I'm lost with Christ in God, hidden with my blessed Lord, while I walk this earthly sod**</u>" (L.C. Hail)